Part II:

House Calls 101

The Complete Clinician's Guide
To In-Home Health Care, Telemedicine
Services, and Long-Distance Treatment
For a Post-Pandemic World

Dr. Scharmaine Lawson, NP

Part II:

House Calls 101

The Complete Clinician's Guide
To In-Home Health Care, Telemedicine
Services, and Long-Distance Treatment
For a Post-Pandemic World

Dedication

—◆—

Dear Skylar & Wyatt. You're my S1S2. My Why. Thank you for giving Mommy the room and space to create. It's an honor sharing life, love, and memories with you.

Foreword

The COVID-19 pandemic has remarkably influenced all of us and, of course, made home visiting very difficult and more challenging. Most home health care providers are offering visits remotely or have started reduced, socially distant, in-person home visits. However, experts in the home health care industry are still working to figure out the ideal way to meet the needs of patients, taking into consideration their access and concerns regarding technology.

An important feature of this book is that it does not have a textbook structure, so you don't need to read in the given sequence of chapters to understand the book. In fact, you can start your journey of the House Call 101 from any chapter based on your interests and preferences.

The updated version of the House Call 101 comprises four sections. The first section has the standard guidelines about what to do before, during, and after conducting an in-home visit. This section is intended to provide an overview of infection control to home-based health care providers. The second section is probably the most important portion of the book since it covers telehealth services and benefiting from remote visits amidst the COVID-19 public health emergency. This section is specially designed to provide a basic understanding for house call health care providers in the application of telehealth services for their patients following the expansion of reimbursement options amidst the COVID-19 pandemic.

The third section is designed for home-based primary care (HBPC) providers and practice staff to support them in understanding the advanced coding opportunities beyond E/M (Evaluation and Management) CPT codes that are available, depending on the greater level of complexity of a patient's requirements. These advanced codes should be aligned with the care provided and facilitate providers in maximizing their Medicare Fee-for-Service reimbursements. The final section is about the Assertive community treatment and the home health care psychiatric services. This section also contains the billing and reimbursement opportunities for the Psychiatric Collaborative Care Management and General Behavioral Health Intervention.

The information and knowledge presented in the book is a wake-up call about why and how an interdisciplinary approach is better than working alone in home health care. We need to understand the major challenges and complexities of home health care during this difficult time. We also need to change our direction and start benefiting from knowledge-based and evidence-based ideas about advanced digital tools and remote patient monitoring technologies recommended by research scientists.

Contents

❧

Dedication 5

Foreword.. 6

Section 1
Home Health Care during
COVID-19 Pandemic

Chapter 1 Origin of the COVID-19: An Overview................. 13

Chapter 2 Providing In-Home Visiting Services amidst the
COVID-19 Public Health Emergency...................................... 21

Section 2
Telemedicine Services: The 2021 House Call

Chapter 3 Introduction 39

Chapter 4 Classification of Telemedicine Services 42

Chapter 5 How to Bill Different Telehealth Services? 50

Chapter 6 Remote Patient Monitoring (RPM): A New Face of Modern Home Health Care 66

Section 3
Advanced Coding Options and
Reimbursement Opportunities

Chapter 7 Transitional Care Management (TCM) 76

Chapter 8 Chronic Care Management (CCM) 80

Chapter 9 Principle Care Management (PCM) 88

Chapter 10 Advance Care Planning (ACP) 90

Chapter 11 Prolonged Services without Contacting the Patient Directly 93

Chapter 12 Prolonged Services with Contacting the Patient Directly 96

Chapter 13 Cognitive Evaluation and Care Plan Services 98

Chapter 14 Counseling Services Regarding Smoking Cessation 101

Chapter 15 Screening, Brief Intervention, and Referral to Treatment (SBIRT) Services 104

Chapter 16 Anticoagulation Management 108

Chapter 17 General Behavioral Health Integration (BHI) and
Care Management Services 110

Chapter 18 Interprofessional Internet Consultation Services 115

Section 4
Assertive Community Treatment and Home
Health Care Psychiatric Services

Chapter 19 Assertive Community Treatment (ACT) 118

Chapter 20 Home Health Care Psychiatric Services............... 125

Chapter 21 Billing and Reimbursement opportunities for the
Psychiatric CoCM and General BHI 129

Section 5
The Future of Home Health Care

References 137

Section

1

Home Health Care during COVID-19 Pandemic

Chapter

1

Origin of the COVID-19: An Overview

Everyone noticed the silence of the social life and daily routine amidst the COVID-19 public health emergency. It was recommended to stay at home and out of crowded places. We experienced some unexpected scenes of empty streets, closed factories and businesses, closed shops and restaurants, mask-covered faces, and suspended flight operations from airlines. There were no concerts, festivals, or sporting events. In fact, we are still living in the fear of getting sick and almost every aspect of our routine life has been changed with the addition of the "NEW NORMAL (Morens et al., 2020).

These are truly unprecedented times, especially for geriatrics and the handicapped. It is hard to remember that no one had heard about "Stay-at-home" or "Social distancing" two or three years ago. The idea of governments recommending their citizens to quarantine at home once seemed like an imaginary movie plot. But then an extremely contagious novel virus—COVID-19 virus —ripped all over the globe and left its impacts on everything in almost no time.

The initial cases of COVID-19 were first reported in Wuhan, China at the end of 2019 (Shereen et al., 2020). Since then, the number of COVID-19 cases have exponentially increased all over the world. The health authorities of the United States confirmed the first COVID-19 case (a 35-year-old man) in Washington State on January 19, 2020 (History.com Editors, 2021). The affected COVID-19 man had returned from Wuhan, China in January 2020 and had a 4-day history of cough and subjective fever. The World Health Organization (WHO) officially announced COVID-19 as a pandemic on March 11th, 2020.

From December 2019 to August 2020, more than 219 million COVID-19 cases have been reported worldwide, including more than 4.55 million deaths. During the same period, more than 40 million cases were reported in the United States, including more than 666,000 deaths (Statista, 2021).

What is COVID-19 and Corona Virus?

COVID-19 (Corona Virus Disease 2019) is a highly communicable disease caused by a novel coronavirus that primarily affects the lungs and airways. COVID-19 virus is a member of the Coronavirus family of viruses, which is one of the largest families of viruses causing mild to severe illnesses in humans. The major clinical feature of the Coronavirus family is the common cold. However, unlike the common cold, the COVID-19 virus is a novel virus of the Coronavirus family, which is extremely contagious and may cause life-threatening illnesses (Shereen et al., 2020). There is no exact treatment yet for COVID-19; only symptomatic treatment and vaccination are administered.

Most individuals recover from COVID-19 without any specific intervention. Some individuals with COVID-19 may not show any specific symptoms (Fever, cough, shortness of breath, and loss of sense of smell); but even if someone has mild symptoms or no symptoms at all, they can still transmit the virus to others. Therefore, social distancing is recommended during the pandemic.

The major and most common symptoms of COVID-19 may include:

- Continuous cough (new-onset)

- High-grade fever
- Loss or change to a sense of taste or smell
- Shortness of breath
- Other less common and nonspecific symptoms may include headache, fatigue, body pain, and sore throat

COVID-19 started as just a quiet ripple of waves. Initially, just a few cases were reported with pneumonia-like features but, by the end of January, almost 100 cases across 19 countries and 4 continents were reported. At that time there was no serious threat of what was about to come next, but it was soon confirmed that the virus is very different from what had been experienced before. The virus proved highly contagious. It attacks not only the lungs, but also other vital organs such as the heart, liver, kidney, and brain.

The symptoms of COVID-19 are very much inconsistent, nonspecific, and wide-ranging. Sometimes a patient shows high-grade fever, complete loss of smell, or respiratory failure. On the other hand, some patients may also have no visible clinical features at all. These inconsistencies are not limited to any specific ages, geographies, or genders. However, geriatric age groups and individuals with immune pathologies and other chronic problems are at the greatest risk of having the worst outcome.

Some Do's and Don'ts to Avoid Getting or Spreading the Virus: The Patient Education during House Calls

Healthcare professionals, including NP's and PA's, must educate their clients during their home visits about the following steps in order to reduce the risk of getting or spreading the infection:

Do's

- Handwashing for at least 20 seconds with water and soap

- If water and soap are not available, hand sanitizer should be used

- Wash hands, especially when getting back at home from outside

- Use of face mask with a proper covering of the nose and mouth

- Covering the nose and mouth with a tissue or sleeve (do not use hands) when sneezing or coughing

- Used tissues should be placed in a bin and hands should be washed immediately

Don'ts

- Don't touch the nose, eyes, and mouth if hands are not washed with water and soap or sanitizer

- Don't break the standard operating practice for self-isolation, social distancing, and social shielding.

Before a house call visit, you must know about any vulnerable patients who may get COVID-19. The high-risk people for contracting COVID-19 are individuals who:

- Have chronic lung problems, such as COPD, asthma, and Cystic Fibrosis

- Have blood or bone marrow cancer

- Are taking different types of cancer therapies

- Have a history of organ transplant

- Are taking medications (low doses of steroids) that may weaken their immune system

- Have a chronic renal disease or are on dialysis

- Are pregnant with serious cardiac problems

- Are 60 years or older

- Have diabetes

- Have chronic liver disease

- Are obese

- Have serious nerves problems such as Multiple Sclerosis, Parkinson's Disease, Cerebral Palsy, and Motor Neuron Disease

Home Health Care Practice and Current COVID-19 Crises

Due to the current COVID-19 pandemic, most of the homebound patients with minor health problems like back pain, indigestion, constipation, allergies, and acne, etc. are unable to see their primary care physicians, nurse practitioners, therapists, and osteopaths. On the other hand, most spinal care physicians/surgeons, orthopedic surgeons, rheumatologists, neurosurgeons and pain management physicians have been offering limited services for critical or emergency patients (*The Home Health Sector Responds to the COVID-19 Crisis*, 2020).

Unfortunately, back pain and other minor health problems for those homebound patients are getting worse during the social distancing and lockdown phases. These individuals are experiencing severe emotional problems and having to deal with discomfort, disability, and disruption of their social life in the current crisis. The homebound patients are becoming more anxious and depressed and feeling neglected. They are not sure how to deal with these symptoms. They are unable to meet their primary care providers even for medical advice on what to do for their minor symptoms that don't necessarily require a traditional in-person, office-based, medical visit.

Undoubtedly, COVID-19 has disrupted everyone's life to some extent, but its impact on homebound patients who are experiencing minor health problems has been disproportionately large.

> *The word "pandemic" is derived from the Greek word "pan" which means "all" and "demos" means "people".*

Chapter

2

Providing In-Home Visiting Services amidst the COVID-19 Public Health Emergency

If you are visiting people in their homes to render home health services, it is highly recommended that you get vaccinated. Most companies are mandating the vaccine for their employees. If you have been vaccinated against COVID-19 and it has been a minimum of two weeks since your final dose of vaccine (sufficient time period for your body to establish immunity), you now have immunity against infection. However, we still don't have enough knowledge about how vaccines will affect the COVID-19 spread. Always follow the standard recommendations as given below while visiting people in their homes to render home health services during the COVID-19 PHE (public health emergency):

Don't conduct home visits if:

- You have any signs and symptoms of COVID-19 (Fever, headache, cough, difficulty breathing, muscle pain, chills, sore throat, and loss of smell or taste)

- You had a positive COVID-19 test and you are still in the period of self-isolation

- You were close to or had contact with someone who has a positive COVID-19 test

- If you are above 65 or/and have other health problems that could make getting COVID-19 even worse, like diabetes, asthma, or hypertension and you still have not completed vaccination

- If you are unable to be vaccinated in certain cases, consider avoiding visits others in their homes

- Remember, not everybody with COVID-19 has visible symptoms but they can still spread the virus without displaying symptoms

- The individual you are visiting in the home has a positive COVID-19 test, is experiencing

COVID-19 symptoms, or is in quarantine due to being in close contact with somebody with positive COVID-19

Before Organizing an In-Home Visit

Before conducting an in-home visit, especially amidst the COVID-19 PHE, you should review and refresh your knowledge regarding the standard recommendations for prevention against getting or spreading the infection. You must review the CDC's latest recommendations on infection prevention and control (IPC) priorities as well as standard and transmission-based precautions related to the COVID-19 (*Healthcare Workers*, 2020).

Immediately cancel home visits if you or anyone in the home:

- Is showing symptoms

- Has tested positive for the COVID-19 test

- Has been in contact with somebody who has tested positive for COVID-19 within the last two weeks

- Is still waiting for their COVID-19 test results

Things to Remember while Preparing for The Home Visit

- Try to obtain as much information as possible before starting the visit and get ready to take proper infection control precautions. Examples of these precautionary measures include the following:

  ➢ Does your back office or scheduling staff ask relevant questions when scheduling or confirming appointments to recognize potential risks and "red flags" that suggest PPE (Personal Protective Equipment) precautions must be taken?

    ▪ This includes identifying caregivers, patients, and family members or any other member in the household who has been outside of the United States within the last 30 days. It also includes inquiring about whether the patient has ever positively tested for TB or/and whether the caregiver, patient, family members, or any other member in the home is ill.

  ➢ Is your scheduling staff or/and front office aware of your proper infection control procedures and policies (e.g., COVID-19, bed bug policy)?

➤ Is the electronic medical record checked before the visit?

- If a provider is showing COVID-19 symptoms, or/and could infect others, home visits must obviously be rescheduled.

- Arrange the medical bag and supplies as given below:

Medical Bag

▪ Arrange the bag before time to facilitate "used" and "cleaned" supplies to be stored separately.

▪ Disinfect the medical bag itself and all supplies that are going into it properly before and after the visit.

▪ In the vehicle, try to place the bag inside a large, clear plastic and high-sided container, if available. If a high-sided container is not available in your vehicle, you can place the bag on a dry, clean surface in the vehicle.

▪ Keep your medical bag out of sight in a locked vehicle whenever possible while traveling.

▪ At the day's end, take your medical bag back

into the office or other established location
to be cleaned and wiped down and to avoid
extreme temperatures.

Supplies

- Always bring a sufficient supply of zippered
  plastic bags of different sizes along with
  plastic disposable bags or disposable
  underpads.

- Always carry the appropriate PPE such as
  gloves, gowns, eye protection, masks, shoe
  covers, and a change of clothes.

- Bring a hand sanitizer or/and antibacterial
  gel. You may also bring a pump soap
  dispenser.

- Bring a red, hard-sided "biohazard-labeled"
  container for the disposal of needles,
  syringes, and scalpels. Store the biohazard
  container with a tight lid within an extra
  zippered plastic bag before disposing of it
  when you return to the office.

- Organize and arrange the supplies in the bag
  based on their usage:

Single-Use Items

Arrange single-use supplies in zippered plastic bags after their use and then place them in the patient's outside garbage after providing proper and clear instructions to the patient and other members in the household to not reopen the disposed of bag. Examples of single-use items include alcohol prep pads, disinfectant wipes, paper towels, wound care dressing supplies, and PPEs.

Reusable Items

Properly clean reusable supplies with disinfecting wipes before putting them back into the medical bag. Examples of reusable supplies are a pulse oximeter, blood pressure cuff, thermometer, and other electronic devices.

Immediately Before the Home Visit

- Immediately before going into the home, review relevant information.

- Talk to the person or family you are planning to visit to explain to them you will be strictly following the COVID-19 PHE public health guidance to minimize risk.

- Discuss your risk mitigation approach and explain it is to protect them and you.

- Arrange and organize the equipment you will require during your visit.

- Ensure that you understand how to use PPE to make it more efficient and avoid unintended risks.

- If you use PPE that definitely obstructs your face, clarify to the person/family why you are using it ahead of your arrival if possible, or upon arrival if essential.

- Make sure you have a clear understanding of where to dispose of any protective equipment after the visit as per public health guidance.

- Make sure to wash your hands using hand sanitizer before and immediately after your visit by following public health guidance.

- You will also require an easy way to contact that person or persons, such as by mobile phone.

- Make sure your team or line manager is aware of your whereabouts and contacts you if you are returning late.

- Review the plan with your team or line manager to ensure that infection risks are minimized and reasonably managed.

During the Home Visit

After assessing risks and recognizing that an in-home visit is essential, follow these precautions:

- Wash your hands with water and soap for a minimum of 20 seconds or use a hand sanitizer that has at least 60% alcohol before entering the home (*Coronavirus Disease 2019 (COVID-19)*, 2020).

- Your first task is to perform daily temperature and symptoms checks, especially before entering the home.

- Immediately screen participants upon arrival. Inquire of the participant or household members if there is the presence of possible symptoms and signs, if there have been possible exposures, and ask about their recent travel and visitors.

- Only carry necessary supplies, materials, and equipment.

- Limit contact with other family members and keep at least two meters distance and follow the public health guidelines about minimizing the COVID-19 infection.

- During your visit, minimize touching the surfaces and avoid putting your personal items down on any surfaces.

- Don't touch your eyes or face, ask for proper ventilation of the room through an open door and window.

- Always wear a cloth face covering or face mask and other essential PPE.

- Keep your visit as concise as possible. If you feel that the risks are inappropriate or unable to manage during the visit, explain and discuss with the patient or family why you need to conclude the visit. Also, discuss the follow-up plan.

Upon entering the home, place your medical bag in a dry, clean area in the home. The disposable underpad or plastic garbage bag you carried may also be used as a barrier for your medical bag. Place the bag high enough off the ground to keep it out of reach of children and to avoid any contamination by animals. Place your tablet or laptop on a clean, dry surface. Wipe off the case and keyboard of your electronic devices with a disinfecting wipe. Put the disposed wipe in a zippered plastic bag with other single-use items and then place them in the patient's outside garbage after providing proper and clear instructions to the patient and other members in the household not to reopen the disposed of bags.

You may choose to sit close to the patient if a dry,

clean surface is available (You may also utilize one of your disposable underpads if required). If essential, choose to stand near the patient rather than sitting, to avoid possible contamination of your personal clothing. You may also consider carrying a portable stool or lightweight chair along with you to sit on during patient visits. It's ideal to sit on plastic or hardwood chairs instead of fabric ones since they are not likely to become contaminated or infested by bed bugs.

Disinfect reusable items by cleaning them with disinfecting wipes before putting them back into the medical bag. Make sure that hazardous materials are disposed of in the biohazard-labeled containers with a tight lid within an extra zippered plastic bag to avoid spills or contamination. Do not place them on open surfaces within the patient's home such as a chair or table. If you are collecting blood in vacutainer tubes, put the blood specimen into a zippered plastic bag. Immediately label the specimen for proper and accurate processing. Wash your hands with soap and water or use your hand sanitizer or antibacterial gel after clean-up.

Application of PPE during the Home Visit

Personal Protective Equipment (PPE) is specialized equipment used for protection against infectious materials. PPE prevents direct contact with body fluid or infectious materials by developing an appropriate barrier between the health care provider and potentially infectious material.

Medical PPE includes gloves, gowns or coverall, face protection, face shield or mask and goggles, head cover, and rubber boots (*Healthcare Workers*, 2020b).

A. Gloves

Gloves protect you when you are directly handling contaminated surfaces or potentially infectious materials. Gloves should be changed when visibly soiled, punctured or torn. Wash your hands upon removing gloves. It should be remembered that gloves cannot replace the need for proper handwashing. Gloves should be used as a component of infection prevention and control (IPC) priorities as well as standard and transmission-based precautions related to the COVID-19.

B. Gown or Coverall

Always wear a gown or coverall when rendering care to patients in their homes, especially in the midst of COVID-19. It should also be used when there is a risk of direct contact with body fluids, blood, and/or potentially infectious materials.

C. Face Protection

Masks should completely cover the mouth and nose

and prevent the penetration of any fluid. Masks should be positioned snuggly over the mouth and nose. Masks may also contain a flexible nose piece and may be secured to the head with elastic or string ties. It is significant to understand multiple different types of masks along with their recommended usage. It should be remembered that not all filtering facepieces (FFP) and masks provide the same protection; therefore, you should understand the limitations and usage of each one.

The use of a face mask is usually not sufficient to provide complete protection. The CDC recommends face masks should be combined with other measures or/ and PPEs accordingly. During home visits, providers and participants should wear a proper, well-fitting face mask or an appropriate cloth face covering. If it requires removal and storage of a cloth face covering or face mask for future use, store in a clean, dry, and sealable paper bag or breathable container. Wash container before its reuse and dispose of storage paper bags frequently.

N95 or FFP2 masks: N95 and FFP2 masks are examples of PPE that protect the wearer from tiny airborne particles as well as from liquid contaminating the face. An FFP2 mask is a form of disposable dust mask that provides moderate protection and is often used for moderate level fine dust/water or oil-based mists, sanding, plastering, and wood dust.

D. Eye Protection (Goggles, Face shields)

Goggles

Goggles should fit snuggly around and over the eyes. A proper fit provides a complete barrier and protects the eyes.

Face Shield

When skin protection is needed in addition to nose, mouth, and eye protection, such as when suctioning copious secretions or irrigating a wound, a face shield is an ideal device to use as a substitute to wearing goggles or a mask. The face shield should properly cover the forehead, extending below the chin and wrapping around the side of the face.

Always use eye protection in the form of goggles or face shields when delivering your home care services to a participant with suspected or confirmed COVID-19. Try not to touch or adjust eye protection while rendering care. Always disinfect and clean eye protection by using recommended methods after removal. Store cleaned eye protection in a clean, dry, and sealable paper bag or breathable container after removal. Wash container before its reuse and dispose of storage paper bags frequently.

E. Respiratory Protection

Respiratory protection should be used via face masks as well as respirators.

N95 respirators are recommended when delivering home care services to a participant with suspected or confirmed COVID-19. Wearers need to be medically fit to wear this type of mask. If the wearer is not fit for this type of mask, a well-fitting surgical face mask should be used instead.

Powered air-purifying respirators (PAPR) are recommended for high-risk aerosol-producing procedures. It is a battery-powered and more complicated filtration system composed of a full-face mask, a power battery-operated blower, a breathing tube, and particulate filters like HEPA filters.

A PAPR is recommended for use if:

- The N95 respirator is not available or does not fit

- If the wearer has a facial deformity or facial hair that would interfere with an N95 respirator or mask-to-face seal

- For a high-risk aerosol-producing procedure

- Delivering your home care services to a participant with suspected or confirmed COVID-19

If you are providing services in the home setting, implementing CDC standard infection control guidelines can help you and your participants and their household members to stay safe while making in-home visits amidst the COVID-19 pandemic.

After Completing a Home Visit

Disinfect and Clean

- All equipment, supplies and materials carried, used, or removed from the home must be disinfected and cleaned properly.

- Wash your hands with water and soap for a minimum of 20 seconds or use a hand sanitizer containing at least 60% alcohol.

- Clean and disinfect the outside of your medical bag by using an appropriate disinfecting wipe when you return to the office. Always dispose of these used wipes according to your infection control procedures.

- Empty the biohazard containers into the appropriate receptacle at the office when they are almost 2/3 full.

Dispose and Preserve PPE

- Remove your PPE just outside of the home. Preserve them, if possible, and dispose of any PPE that is damaged or soiled.

- Always follow public health guidelines immediately after the visit.

- At the day's end, remove and wash your clothes that may have been exposed to the virus.

2

Telemedicine Services:
The 2021 House Call

Chapter

3

Introduction

O ne of the golden lines in the terror of the
COVID-19 pandemic is the evolution and rapid
advancements of telemedicine. According to the CMS,
"Telemedicine is the exchange of medical details from one
site to another via electronic communication to improve
a patient's health". The term telemedicine is a general
umbrella term for the application of Information and
Communication Technologies (ICT) in health-related
processes and services. Telemedicine refers to the ICT-
supported provision of health services while healthcare
providers and patients are not present at the same place.
In this context, ensuring secure transmission of text,

voice, and image-based medical data is a prerequisite in telemedicine services, for medical diagnosis, prevention, treatment, and follow-ups. Since the beginning of the pandemic, telemedicine and online services have greatly proliferated (Khoshrounejad et al., 2021).

Some of the major advantages of telemedicine amidst the pandemic include:

1. Access to care without fear of getting or spreading infection

2. Positive engagement with new patients and continuity of care with established patients

3. Coordination with other consultants

Other advantages include better opportunities for enhanced patient access, house calls, and a better ability to review blood pressure logbooks and medications that might have been forgotten at home during a classic in-person office visit. Relaxation of CMS rules with regards to the COVID-19 pandemic has provided greater regulatory flexibility and an accelerated expansion of the use of telemedicine (Brunton, 2021).

The major modifications made effective after March 2020 for the COVID-19 pandemic include:

1. Reimbursement of virtual visits at the same rate as traditional in-person office visits

2. Payment for professional medical services furnished to beneficiaries in all regions of the country

3. No geographic limitations or restrictions for telemedicine services for established patients

4. Flexibility to use daily video conferencing platforms (i.e., not only those compliant with the HIPAA)

Chapter

Classification of Telemedicine Services

Telemedicine services can be classified into several types depending on the communication mode, timing of information transmitted, and consultation purpose.

1. Mode of communication

2. Timing of information transmitted

3. Purpose of consultation

Telemedicine Services According to the Mode of Communication

Multiple different technologies can be used based on the mode of communication to deliver efficient telehealth services. The four primary modes of communication are audio, video, text, and emails.

A. Video

- Telemedicine facility visits
- Apps
- Video on chat platforms,
- Skype/Face Time

B. Audio

- Phone calls
- Apps
- VoIP (Voice over internet protocol)

C. Text-based

- Online chat-based applications (smartphone apps, websites, and other internet-based chat systems)
- General text/messaging/chat platforms (WhatsApp, Google Hangouts, Facebook Messenger).

D. Email/Fax

A. Video-based Telehealth Services

Online video-based communication has greatly expanded telehealth services, especially amidst the COVID-19 public health emergency (PHE). With an internet connection and a webcam, you can now arrange a virtual face-to-face visit with your patient. In video-based telehealth services you can perform virtual inspection services of your patient, especially the affected body regions, and suggest a provisional diagnosis. Examples of video-based telehealth services include telemedicine facility visits, apps (Zoom, GoToMeeting), video on chat platforms, and Skype/FaceTime, etc.

B. Audio-based Telehealth Services

Telehealth services can be provided via audio calls by using a mobile phone, different audio apps, and even VoIP (voice over internet protocol). It is the fastest way of communication between a patient to a healthcare professional, between two healthcare professionals who need to discuss complicated issues, and between a clinician to a caregiver for detailed medical discussion. It is also known as tele-triage.

C. Text-based Telehealth Services

In text-based telehealth services, the conversation between a healthcare professional and a patient is made in the form of text messaging. It includes specialized chat-based smartphone apps, websites, text messages (SMS), and internet messaging systems like WhatsApp, Google Hangouts, and Facebook messenger, etc.

D. Email/Fax (Store-and-Forward)

Your patients may use email/fax to share their reports and communicate about their current health status, receive reminders about their health appointments and preventative care, and stay up-to-date about their medical findings. Healthcare professionals may use this mode of communication to share patient medical data, especially recorded videos, photos, and reports with other providers at other locations and to develop appropriate treatment plans for the patient. For example, a physician at a small clinic may use the email system to share a patient's MRI or CT scan to a radiologist at a distant location to confirm the diagnosis.

Telemedicine Services According to the Timing of Information Transmitted

The goal of telehealth services is to eliminate the distance barrier and facilitate medical access for everyone, which would otherwise not be available, especially amid the COVID-19 PHE and in remote communities. Telehealth is basically the transmission of voice, image, data, and information rather than moving patients or healthcare providers. These images, data, voices, and information may be transmitted in real-time or store-and-forward modes. Based on the timing of information transmitted, telehealth services can be classified as:

A. Synchronous telehealth services (Real-time mode)

B. Asynchronous telehealth services (Store-and-forward mode)

A. *Synchronous Mode*

It is the "live-video conferencing" or "live audio communication" which is "two-way audio-visual communication" between a patient and a healthcare professional. In synchronous mode, both the patient and the healthcare provider are present at the same time during their communication, which allows real-time interaction between them. It includes real-time video/audio/text interaction to exchange relevant information for proper diagnosis, medication prescription, and counseling.

B. *Asynchronous Mode*

It is the store-and-forward mode of communication in which data is transmitted without the need for real-time interaction between a patient and the healthcare provider. In asynchronous telehealth services, data is locally captured, then stored temporarily and eventually transferred later via a website or email/fax. The billing provider then reviews the stored data to make a diagnosis, suggest relevant treatment, and provide recommendations. It includes the upload of images (X-ray or MRI), files, and data through a secure website and sharing of data through emails or fax.

Telehealth services According to the Purpose of the Consultation

A. For Non-Emergency Cases

For all non-emergency cases, there are two types of patient consultations:

a) First consultation

b) Follow-up consultation

a) First Consultation

The first consult is the first communication between a patient and a billing physician for diagnosis, treatment, and counseling.

First consultation means:

The patient is communicating the first time with the healthcare provider.

OR

The person has communicated with the healthcare provider, but more than six months have passed since the last communication.

OR

The patient is communicating for any new condition with the healthcare provider.

A healthcare provider may have limited understanding about the patient seeking the first consultation through telehealth services such as voice or text-based modes; however, if the first consult happens via a video-based mode of communication, the healthcare provider can make better judgments and provide better recommendations, including prescribing medicines.

b) Follow-up Consult

Follow-up consult means the patient is communicating with the same healthcare provider within six months of his/her previous visit and this is for the continuation of care of the same health condition.

B. For Emergency Cases

Telehealth services are usually not recommended for emergency cases when in-person medical care is available; however, in the case where traditional in-person medical care is not available, telehealth resources might be the only way to provide timely care. For emergency cases, telehealth services should be limited to first aid, life-saving measures, and advice for a referral. In all emergency cases, the patient must be referred for an in-person medical visit as soon as possible.

Chapter

5

How to Bill Different Telehealth Services?

H ome healthcare professionals need to understand the updated guidelines about the use of telehealth services following the expansion of reimbursement opportunities amidst the COVID-19 public health emergency. The CMS (Centers for Medicare and Medicaid Services) has demonstrated some specific coverage prerequisites for what they consider CMS telehealth services (Brunton, 2021).

CMS continues to provide increased opportunities and regulatory relaxation for providers to use appropriate technology for their patients, including telephone Evaluation & Management (E/M) services, video visits, virtual check-ins, remote assessment or evaluation of videos and photos, E-visits or online digital E/M services, and remote patient monitoring (RPM) services. Before the Public Health Emergency (PHE) of the COVID-19 pandemic, Medicare would cover telehealth services just for those patients located in a rural healthcare professional shortage area (HPSA) or a region outside of a metropolitan statistical area (MSA). In addition, Medicare also required the patient to travel to an "originating site" (approved healthcare facility) to receive the telehealth service from a distant site provider.

In response to the COVID-19 Public Health Emergency and to support healthcare providers in the fight against COVID-19, the Coronavirus Preparedness and Response Supplemental Appropriations Act (CPRSAA) and other legislation was signed into law. Under these emergency actions, multiple different telehealth waivers temporarily allow patients to receive telemedicine services regardless of their approved locations. CMS also waived the distant and originating site prerequisites temporarily and started to pay for virtual services at the same rate as traditional in-person care (Rogers, 2021). Eligible healthcare professionals who can provide virtual care and bill for their telehealth services during the COVID-19 PHE may include:

- Physicians
- Nurse Practitioners
- Physician Assistants
- Nurse-Midwives
- Certified Registered Nurse Anesthetist
- Clinical Psychologists
- Licensed Clinical Social Workers
- Registered Dieticians
- Nutrition Professionals
- Physical Therapists
- Occupational Therapists
- Speech-language Pathologists

Virtual Care and Reimbursement Options

Video Visits

If a telehealth visit is organized via a two-way video and audio telecommunication method allowing real-time communication between the patient and the provider, the service can be reported using the home E/M codes i.e., CPT 99341- 99345 and CPT 99347-99350, and domiciliary E/M codes i.e., CPT 99327-99328 and CPT 99334-99337. You will report the Place of Service (POS) to demonstrate where the visit would have taken place face-to-face e.g., POS 12 home.

Telephone (Audio-Only) Services

During the COVID-19 public health emergency, Medicare will provide reimbursement for certain services when delivered using telephone calls to facilitate patients who may not have resources for participating in a video visit. Telephone or Audio-only services may include:

CPT 99441: CPT 99441 is recommended for telephone E/M service provided by a physician or other qualified healthcare provider who may report E/M services delivered to an established patient, guardian, or parent that neither originates from a relevant evaluation and management service provided within the past seven days nor led to an evaluation and management service within the next 24 hours or earliest available appointment, 5-10 minutes of clinical conversation.

CPT 99442: CPT 99442 should be used for telephone E/M service provided by a physician or other qualified healthcare provider who may report E/M services delivered to an established patient, guardian, or parent that neither originated from a relevant evaluation and management service provided within the past seven days nor led to an evaluation and management service within the next 24 hours or earliest available appointment, 11-20 minutes of clinical conversation.

CPT 99443: CPT 99443 is recommended for telephone E/M service provided by a physician or other qualified healthcare provider who may report E/M services delivered to an established patient, guardian, or parent that neither originated from a relevant evaluation and management service provided within the past seven days nor led to an evaluation and management service within the next 24 hours or earliest available appointment, 21-30 minutes of clinical conversation.

The telephone evaluation and management codes above represent a medical discussion that can be billed only by physicians, clinical nurse specialists, physician assistants, nurse practitioners, and certified nurse midwives having E/M within their approved scope of practice.

Telephone Services Prerequisites

For telephone or audio-only E/M services, the healthcare professional must need to meet the following requirements:

- Telephone or audio-only E/M visits must be initiated by patients, although CMS has explained that providers may require first educating their patients on the availability of this service.

- CMS is temporarily considering telephone CPT codes 99441, 99442, and 99443 to be a "Medicare telehealth service" and providers need to be using modifier 95 to demonstrate the service as telehealth for traditional Medicare billing.

Non-Physician Practitioners

Other eligible and qualified health care providers, including nurse practitioners, clinical psychologists, physical therapists, licensed clinical social workers, speech-language pathologists, and occupational therapists can report Telephone E/M services to bill for telehealth services using the following CPT codes:

CPT 98966: CPT 98966 is recommended for telephone E/M service provided by a non-physician healthcare provider who may report E/M services delivered to an established patient, guardian, or parent, that neither originated from a relevant evaluation and management service provided within the past seven days nor led to an evaluation and management service within the next 24 hours or earliest available appointment, 5-10 minutes of clinical conversation.

CPT 98967: CPT 98967 should be used for telephone E/M service provided by a non-physician healthcare provider who may report E/M services, delivered to an established patient, guardian, or parent, that neither originated from a relevant evaluation and management service provided within the past seven days nor led to an evaluation and management service within the next 24 hours or earliest available appointment, 11-20 minutes of clinical conversation.

CPT 98968: CPT 98968 is recommended for telephone E/M service provided by a non-physician healthcare provider who may report E/M services, delivered to an established patient, guardian, or parent, that neither originated from a relevant evaluation and management service provided within the past seven days nor led to an evaluation and management service within the next 24 hours or earliest available appointment, 21-30 minutes of clinical conversation.

Other Audio Only Services

CMS has also decided to provide reimbursement for counseling, psychotherapy, education, and nutrition and therapy services via audio-only services. Following is a list of services related to home-based care. You can check the detailed Medicare's List of Telehealth Services for a comprehensive understanding of Medicare audio-only services (*List of Telehealth Services | CMS*, 2021).

1. Advance Care Planning (ACP)

CPT 99497 (at least 16 minutes) and CPT 99498 (minimum of 46 minutes) should be used for billing Advance Care Planning services. ACP service needs a clinical discussion by an eligible qualified healthcare provider discussing advance directives or end-of-life priorities with the patient or/and caregiver.

2. *Annual Wellness Visits*

HCPCS G0438 and G0439 are recommended for Annual Wellness Visits through audio-only technology.

3. *Smoking Cessation Services*

CPT 99406 and 99407 should be used for smoking cessation services by audio-only technology.

4. HCPCS G0396 and G0397are recommended for structured assessment as well as brief intervention services related to alcohol or/and substance abuse (except for tobacco) through audio-only technology.

5. For annual alcohol misuse screening and counseling, the recommended codes are HCPCS G0442 and G0443.

6. HCPCS G0506 should be used for chronic care management (CCM) services; however, it should be remembered that this service can only be used a single time for new patients or for those patients not seen within a 12-month period when first enrolled in CCM.

Important Considerations

Physical Examination

Physical Exams through telehealth are limited, but it is possible and permitted for a provider to document specific observations such as skin lesions or color, rashes, respiration quality, evidence of dyspnea or wheezing, and vital signs as described by the patient. When this is performed, these factors may also participate in the level of coding.

Documentation Requirements

Providers should document telehealth visits similarly to the way they would document classic in-person visits. E/M coding needs documentation of a Chief Complaint, History of present illness (HPI), review of systems (ROS), PFSH (past medical, family, and social history), physical examination, clinical decision making, and assessment and plan. It should be remembered that for established patients, just two out of the three E/M elements (i.e., history, physical exam, clinical decision making) are needed to assist the level of service.

Privacy

During the COVID-19 public health emergency, the U.S. Health Department has announced some relaxation in HIPAA regulations so that providers can use platforms such as Facebook Messenger video chat, Apple FaceTime, Zoom, Google Hangouts video, or Skype, etc., as acceptable tools of two-way video and audio telecommunications. Remember, no public-facing apps such as Twitch, Facebook Live, or TikTok are allowed.

Technology

Many Medicare telehealth services need interactive video and audio telecommunications allowing real-time communication between the patient and the provider at home. The only exception is for audio-only services like Advance Care Planning and Telephone E/M.

Communication Technology-Based Services (CTBS)

During the COVID-19 PHE, the following communication technology-based services can be rendered to both new and established patients. CMS thinks the virtual check-in codes can be useful even after the COVID-19 public health emergency when they no longer reimburse audio-only telephone E/M (CPT 99441, 99442, and 99443). However, amidst the public health emergency for audio-only services, providers should consider reporting telephone E/M CPT codes as they provide greater reimbursement than virtual check-in services.

Virtual Check-In (HCPCS G2012 and HCPCS G2252)

- HCPCS G2012 involves at least 5-10-minute and HCPCS G2252 includes a minimum of 11-20 minutes of clinical discussion by a qualified healthcare provider with the patient or caregiver, without including clinical staff time.

- The communication can be made audio-only (e.g., telephone) or two-way video.

- During the COVID-19 PHE only, it can be allowed for both new and established patients.

- It is mainly intended to evaluate the patient's condition to confirm if a face-to-face visit is necessary.

- It also needs a patient-initiated call or question.

Assessment of Recorded Video or/and Photo (Image) (HCPCS G2010)

- HCPCS G2010 involves pre-recorded video or/and image of good quality provided by the patient or caregiver

- It needs documentation of advanced consent at least once per year (may be written, electronic, or verbal)

- HCPCS G2010 needs follow-up and

interpretation to the patient or/and caregiver within 24 working hours (follow-up can be made through a patient portal communication, secure text/email, telephone, or two-way video)

- During the COVID-19 PHE only, it can be provided to both new and established patients.

Remote Evaluation of Recorded Video or/and Photo (Image) by a Non-Physician Healthcare Provider (HCPCS G2250)

- HCPCS G2250 involves the reporting from providers without E/M within their recognized scope of practice such as clinical psychologists, physical therapists, licensed clinical social workers, speech-language pathologists, and occupational therapists.

- HCPCS G2250 includes the pre-recorded video or/and image of good quality provided by the patient or caregiver.

- It needs documentation of advanced consent at least once per year (may be written, electronic, or verbal).

- HCPCS G2250 needs follow-up and interpretation to the patient or/and caregiver within 24 working hours (follow-up can be made through a patient portal communication, secure text/email, telephone, or two-way video).

- During the COVID-19 PHE only, this can be provided to both new and established patients

Online Digital E/M Services or E-Visits

Digital communications made through a secure patient portal or any secure platforms (e.g., secure digital applications or secure email) over a seven-day time addressing an acute symptom or problem that does not need a face-to-face or telehealth visit. These services may include the following:

CPT 99421: CPT 99421 should be used for online digital E/M services provided to an established patient from a qualified professional (i.e., physician, physician assistant, nurse practitioner), for up to cumulative seven days, and requires a minimum of 5-10 minutes.

CPT 99422: CPT 99422 is reported for online digital E/M services provided to an established patient from a qualified provider (i.e., physician, physician assistant, nurse practitioner), for up to cumulative seven days, and requires a minimum of 11-20 minutes.

CPT 99423: It is recommended for online digital E/M services delivered for an established patient by a qualified professional (i.e., physician, physician assistant, nurse practitioner), for up to cumulative seven days, and involves 21 minutes or above.

CPT 98970: CPT 98970 is recommended for online digital assessment and management services, rendered to an established patient from a qualified non-physician healthcare provider (i.e., clinical psychologist, licensed clinical social workers, occupational therapist, physical therapists, and speech-language pathologists), for up to cumulative seven days, and requires minimum 5-10 minutes.

CPT 98971: It is used for reporting of online digital assessment and management services provided to an established patient from a qualified non-physician healthcare provider (i.e., clinical psychologist, licensed clinical social workers, occupational therapist, physical therapists, and speech-language pathologists), for up to cumulative seven days, and requires minimum 11-20 minutes.

CPT 98972: Online digital assessment and management, provided to an established patient by a qualified non-physician healthcare professional (i.e., licensed clinical social workers, clinical psychologists, physical therapists, occupational therapists, and speech-language pathologists), for up to cumulative seven days, and requires 21 minutes or above.

Important Considerations

- Do not report online digital evaluation and management services for non-evaluative electronic communications like scheduling appointments or reviewing test results.

- E-visits are patient-initiated communications that cannot be linked to an evaluation and management or previous reportable service for the same issue within the last seven days. Do not report an online digital E/M service if a separately reportable service within the seven-day time occurs for the same issue.

- The seven-day time starts when the provider individually reviews the patient-generated issue and is cumulative over the future seven days when the issue is addressed. It should be remembered that the service time includes reviewing the initial inquiry, reviewing patient medical records or data associated with the problem, individual interaction with other clinical staff associated with the patient's problem, recommendation of management plans, development of prescriptions, ordering of lab investigations, and subsequent communication with the caregiver/patient through online email, telephone, or other digitally supported communication tools.

- All qualified healthcare providers within the same practice group who contribute to the online digital assessment of the same issue contribute to the cumulative service time.

- During COVID-19 public health emergency only, they may be reported for both new and established patients.

- CPT 99453, 99454, 99091, 99457, and 99458 are recommended for remote patient monitoring services, which are explained in the section below.

Chapter

6

Remote Patient Monitoring (RPM): A New Face of Modern Home Health Care

T he remote patient monitoring section is prepared to guide house call programs in the application of RPM services to provide care for their patients following the expansion and accelerated demands for telemedicine resulting from the COVID-19 pandemic. However, it's significant to understand that remote patient monitoring is not separately proposed by the Centers for Medicare and Medicaid Services (CMS) definition; thus, the opportunity to apply for reimbursement using technology for remote patient monitoring services will likely continue after the end of the COVID-19 public health emergency (Prevounce Health, 2021).

Introduction of RPM Services

Remote patient monitoring is defined as the application of technology through medical devices to fetch and analyze patient physiologic data to develop a management plan related to an acute or/ and chronic health problem or illness. The physiologic data such as blood glucose or blood pressure should be collected digitally, which CMS explains as transmitted automatically to the practice. Remote patient monitoring may be billed by qualified healthcare professionals (i.e., physicians, physician assistants, nurse practitioners), but the monitoring and care management services of the management plan may be delivered in coordination with clinical staff under the general supervision of the billing provider. CMS explained that during the COVID-19 PHE, RPM services can be rendered to both new and established patients. At the end of the COVID-19 public health emergency, CMS further explained their policy by stating that an established patient-provider relationship will be necessary to bill RPM services. RPM services require patient consent; however, they may be acquired at the time services are delivered.

RPM Prerequisites

It is significant that qualified healthcare professionals understand all the necessities and what needs to be documented before billing for RPM services. The basic requirements may include the following:

- RPM services must be commenced during a face-to-face encounter or (telehealth during the COVID-19 public health emergency) for patients not seen within the last 12-month period.

- Patient consent is necessary, and it should be documented for RPM services.

- The RPM device should fulfill the FDA's criteria of a "medical device" (it does not have to be essentially approved by the FDA, but it must still fulfill the basic requirements). The medical device is required for the collection and transmission of valid and reliable physiologic data that facilitates understanding of a patient's current health condition to propose and manage a treatment plan (Office of Regulatory Affairs, 2018).

- CMS recommended CPT 99457 and 99458 to render care management services by using interactive communication tools. As with delivering care management services, clinical staff's time related to CPT 99457 and 99458 can be reported under the general supervision of the billing provider. Clinical staff means an individual who provides assistance under the supervision of a physician or other qualified healthcare provider and who is permitted by regulation, law, and facility policy to assist in the performance of a pertinent professional service but does not personally report that specific professional service (Please check the CY 2021 Medicare Physician Fee Schedule Final Rule and CPT codebook for primary reference source).

- A minimum of 16 days of is needed to render and bill for RPM services involving CPT 99453 and 99454; it is recommended that data be collected and transmitted every 30 days. CMS also finalized the 16-day data requirement, and it will remain unchanged in their final policy even after the COVID-19 public health emergency ends.

- RPM services may also be billed in combination with CCM (Chronic Care Management), TCM (Transitional Care Management), and BHI (Behavioral Health Integration) services as long as effort and time are not double-counted.

- Per CY 2021 Medicare Physician Fee Schedule Final Rule and CPT codebook (*CMS*, 2021), you must not count any RPM time on a day or period when the billing provider reports an E/M face-to-face service. Note: During the COVID-19 PHE, CMS relaxed the minimum 16-day requirement to bill for providing RPM services, but the relaxation is just for those patients who have confirmed or suspected COVID-19. In such circumstances, CMS acknowledged the value of short-term monitoring (must be at least for two days) for acute problems and is permitted payment for CPT codes 99453, 99454, 99091, 99457, and 99458.

Some Key Components of RPM Services

RPM Care Episode: RPM care episode initiates when the remote physiologic monitoring service is started and ends with accomplishment of the established treatment goals.

Interactive Communication (Pertinent to CPT 99457 & 99458): A real-time synchronous communication between billing provider or clinical staff and a patient via two-way audio that is capable of being intensified with video or other advanced forms of data transmission.

RPM Care Plan: RPM services include establishing a care plan by assessing and analyzing the patient's data. After the collection of the first month's data, the CMS expects the billing provider to establish a care plan with the patient. The provider then must follow the care plan until the targeted goals are accomplished, which indicates the end of the episode of care.

Remember that according to CMS, CPT 99457 and 99458 are formulated as care management services that need a pertinent care plan for RPM services to be established, monitored, implemented, and revised, and involve the delivery of support services. The care plan may associate with one or more chronic issues that are monitored remotely and can be delivered under general supervision. "General supervision" means that in certain conditions when the billing provider does not personally provide the service, it is still delivered under his/her proper control and direction. However, his/her physical presence is not needed. The timing and sequence of when to report the several RPM codes may be confusing. The following is a recommended timeline of the sequence of billing for certain RPM codes outlined in CY 2021 Medicare Physician Fee Schedule Final Rule:

CPT 99453: CPT 99453 should be reported during the initial calendar month of the commencement of the RPM service. It reflects clinical staff time that involves discussions with a caregiver or/and patient on how to use one or more medical devices (Must be billed only once per care episode).

CPT 99454: CPT 99454 is reported at the end of the month once you have at least 16 days of patient physiologic data. It is also recommended for supplying the medical device to the patient which digitally and automatically transmits physiologic data to the provider's office (once per every 30 days period).

CPT 99091: After collection of the first 30 days of physiologic data, if the provider consumes at least 30 minutes (all billing provider time) indirect patient time for analyzing and reviewing that data to establish treatment plans and/or developing or discussing the RPM specific care plan with the caregiver/patient, then this code can be submitted.

CPT 99457: CPT 99457 is recommended for care management service and should be reported only once you have a minimum of 16 days of the patient's data and have established an RPM-specific care plan for the caregiver/patient. This is purely a time-based code that involves at least 20 minutes of billing provider and clinical staff time. CPT 99457 requires interactive communication with the caregiver/patient and is for interpreting, monitoring, and communicating with the caregiver/patient about the values and physiologic data results.

CPT 99458: CPT 99458 is recommended for care management service. It is an add-on code only that should be used in conjunction with CPT 99457 (at least 40 minutes per calendar month to submit both 99457 & 99458) involving the application of interactive communication with the caregiver/patient by the billing provider or clinical staff.

The Future of the Telehealth Services

Although face-to-face interaction is always important and will never go away; telehealth services have proven to be tremendously valuable and will continue, even after the COVID-19 public health emergency (Kichloo et al., 2020).

An increasingly powerful aspect of telehealth services is RPM (remote patient monitoring), which is the use of portable high-tech devices to track and record patient data from healthcare providers on such matrices as heart rate, glucose levels, blood pressure and blood oxygen levels.

The future of telehealth services is bright, and new virtual technologies are expected to improve continuously and rapidly over the next decade. Researchers are working and developing digital technologies to further optimize virtual medical visits.

Section

3

Advanced Coding Options and Reimbursement Opportunities

This section is designed for home-based primary care (HBPC) providers and practice staff to support them in understanding the advanced coding opportunities beyond E/M (Evaluation and Management) CPT codes that are available depending on the greater level of complexity of patient requirements. These advanced codes should be aligned with the care provided and permit providers to maximize their Medicare Fee-for-Service reimbursements. Please visit the CMS Medicare Learning Network (MLN) for the latest detailed information on updated guidelines (*MLN Home Page | CMS*, 2021).

Chapter

7

Transitional Care Management (TCM)

Transitional Care Management is the supervised care management of Medicare beneficiaries who transition back to their own home, an assisted living facility, a domiciliary, or a rest home from an observation or inpatient hospital stay, rehabilitation center, or skilled nursing facility (*Tools and Tip Sheets*, 2021). Several studies have shown practices that offer a transitional care management model of care minimize unplanned 30-day hospital readmissions by up to 30 percent. Practices may consider implementing the TCM model of care to manage their acute discharge patients to promote more accelerated follow-up, improve care, and achieve positive outcomes.

- TCM services can be delivered to both new and established patients whose clinical or/ and psychosocial issues need moderate to high MDM (medical decision-making) complexity.

- TCM initiates upon the date of discharge of the patient and persists for the next 29 days.

- It needs appropriate documentation of interactive patient communication (can be face-to-face or telephone) with the caregiver and/or patient within two working days of discharge.

- Physicians and non-physician practitioners like Nurse Practitioners (NPs), Physician assistants (PAs) Clinical nurse specialists (CNSs), and Certified nurse-midwives (CNMs) who are legally qualified and authorized to render their services in the state in which services are delivered to the patient, may perform TCM.

- A face-to-face visit with the patient must take place within 7 to 14 business days from discharge.

- CPT 99495 should be reported as the Evaluation and Management code for the post-discharge face-to-face encounter that must take place within 14 business days of discharge and needs moderate medical decision-making complexity.

- CPT 99496 is recommended as the evaluation and management code for a post-discharge face-to-face encounter that must occur within seven business days of discharge and needs high medical decision-making complexity.

- As CMS keeps on improving payment for care management and coordination and finds TCM application low compared to the frequency of Medicare beneficiaries with eligible discharges, they've uncoupled care management services that were earlier considered to be duplicative. TCM services can now report concurrently (i.e., within the same calendar month) as Chronic Care Management (99490, 99491, 99487, 99489, 99439), Advance Care Planning (99497, 99498), Care Plan Oversight (G0181, G0182), Behavioral Health Integration (BHI) services (99484, 99492, 99493, 99494, and G2214), Prolonged Services for both face-to-face and non-face-to-face (99358, 99359), Cognitive Assessment and Care Planning (99483), Inter-professional Consultations (99446, 99447,

99448, 99449, 99451, 99452), Remote Patient Monitoring (99457, 99458), and Principle Care Management Services (G2064, G2065). It is important to make sure time is not "double-counted" for multiple care management services while billing or reporting for TCM and care management services for the same patient within the same calendar month.

Chapter

8

Chronic Care
Management (CCM)

Chronic care management is a vital part of primary care medicine that is extremely helpful in improving health and care for Medicare beneficiaries. Chronic Care Management, as explained by CMS, is a minimum of 20 minutes of combined provider and clinical staff time per calendar month. This time should be devoted to care coordination and the management of chronic problems of patients. Medicare beneficiaries are eligible for Chronic Care Management services if they have at least two or more chronic problems expected to last for a minimum of 12 months or until death. The time of clinical staff must be supervised by a physician or other qualified health care provider, per calendar month. Chronic Care Management also needs a thorough care plan to be developed, monitored, implemented, and revised as required.

- Patient's verbal or written consent is necessary before initiating CCM services. Appropriate documentation of advance consent before starting CCM services may include updating the patient on the availability of Chronic Care Management services and possible applicable cost-sharing like co-pays, that only one provider may bill/deliver Chronic Care Management services during the calendar month, and the right of the patient to end Chronic Care Management services at any time. CMS just needs informed consent to be obtained once before billing for Chronic Care Management services unless there is a billing provider change. Refer to the Care Management webpage seven for additional information.

- Only one qualified and eligible provider (Physician, Physician Assistant, Nurse Practitioner, Clinical Nurse Specialist, and Certified Nurse-Midwife) can provide and be billed or paid for CCM services during a calendar month.

- For patients not seen within one year before the initiation of Chronic Care Management services or new patients, the advanced consent and commencement of services must take place during a face-to-face encounter with the billing provider.

- Eligible patients must have two or more chronic problems that are documented and managed. The chronic problems are expected to last for a minimum of 12 months or until death, and place the patient at acute exacerbation, higher risk of death, or functional decline (e.g., COPD, Alzheimer's dementia, cardiovascular disease).

- Chronic care management requirements that must be offered to enrolled patients in CCM services may include the following:

  - Initiating visit (needed for new patients or patients not seen within 12 months).

  - Recording of patient information in the form of structured data via Certified Electronic Health Record (EHR) Technology.

  - Continuous or 24/7 access and Continuity

of Care (i.e., after-hours on-call availability and professional relationship with a dedicated member of the care team with whom the patient can coordinate and schedule successive routine appointments).

- Comprehensive Care Management services for chronic problems including systematic evaluation of the patient's medical, psychosocial, and functional demands.

- An Electronic Person-Centered Care Plan should be developed. The formal and separate care plan must be developed, monitored, and/or revised as necessary. A copy of the comprehensive care plan must be provided to the caregiver/patient.

- There should be proper Management of Care Transitions.

- There must be appropriate Home and Community Based Care Coordination.

- There should be the establishment of enhanced communication opportunities such as an easy approach to ways of electronic communication other than telephones like secure messaging, patient portals, or other non-face-to-face asynchronous consultation ways.

- Complex CCM (CPT 99487, 99489) needs Medical Decision Making (MDM) of average to severe complexity described by the billing provider.

- CMS explains the CCM comprehensive care plan as a patient-centered electronic care plan depending on the mental, physical, psychosocial, cognitive, environmental, and functional evaluation and an inventory of resources for all health conditions, with a special focus on the chronic problems being managed. A copy of the comprehensive care plan must be provided to the caregiver/patient initially upon the development of the plan. The electronic formal and separate chronic care management plan must be available and accessible within the medical record. It should be shared with relevant members of the care team on time. According to CMS, the comprehensive care plan often includes the following components:

  - List of problems
  - Expected outcome and prognosis
  - Measurable management goals
  - Management of symptoms

- Planned interventions and recognition of individuals who are responsible for each intervention

- Management of medications

- Social and community services were ordered

- A detailed description of how agencies, services, and specialists outside of the practice are directed or coordinated

- Needs a schedule for periodic analysis, and when possible, revisions (consider updating and analyzing the CCM care plan annually as a component of Annual Wellness Visits)

- CPT 99490: Minimum of 20 minutes of the time of clinical staff as supervised by a physician or qualified health care provider per calendar month

- CPT 99439: an add-on code that can only be reported and billed in conjunction with CPT 99490

- CPT 99491: recommended for a minimum of 30 minutes individually performed by the physician or other qualified healthcare provider per calendar month

- CPT 99487: should be reported for complex chronic care management services delivered at a minimum of 60 minutes of clinical staff time as supervised by a physician or qualified health care provider per calendar month

- CPT 99489: recommended for every additional 30 minutes of clinical staff time as supervised by the physician or other qualified health care provider

- HCPCS G0506: should be submitted for comprehensive assessment and care planning by the physician or other qualified health care provider for patients who need chronic care management services. It should be separately billed from monthly care management services. G0506 is billable only once per patient in combination with CCM initiation. This code should only be used for new patients when the billing provider personally engages in direct face-to-face time while creating and discussing the CCM care plan with the caregiver or the patient/caregiver.

- Chronic care management is bundled, which means it cannot be billed within the same calendar month as the below services:

  - Care Plan Oversight (G0181 & G0182)
  - ESRD Services (90951-90970)

- Prolonged Services Non-Face-to-Face (99358, 99359)

- Home and outpatient INR monitoring (93792, 93793)

- Telephone E/M services (99441-99443)

- Analysis of physiologic data (99091)

• Do not submit CPT codes 99487, 99489, 99490, or 99491, within the same calendar month. The provider should choose one type of CCM service that indicates their efforts and time.

• As described in 2020, Medicare Physician Fee Schedule Final Rule, both CCM and TCM services were unbundled and may be billed within the same calendar month for traditional Medicare objectives. However, CPT still considers the CCM and TCM services as bundled, so the policies of commercial payers may vary accordingly.

Chapter

9

Principle Care Management (PCM)

Principle Care Management (PCM) services are almost like chronic care management services. However, these services are much more focused on comprehensive care management for a single high-risk condition of sufficient severity to keep the patient at risk of hospitalization, or this condition must have been the reason for the last hospitalization which lead to the establishment or revision of a disease-specific care plan.

- Patient consent in verbal form is essential and should be documented to inform applicable cost-sharing and to make the patient aware that only one provider can render and bill for principle care management services per calendar month.

- PCM requires an initiating encounter for a new patient that is billed separately.

- When a patient is enrolled in Principle Care Management services, information recording is required in the form of structured data via Certified Electronic Health Record (EHR) Technology, along with 24/7 access (after-hours on-call), condition-specific care management, dedicated and designated care team member, a condition-specific electronic care plan, management of referrals and transitions, community and home-based care coordination, and improved communication opportunities.

- HCPCS G2064: PCM, 30 minutes of healthcare professional time per month for a single high-risk condition. • HCPCS G2065: PCM, 30 minutes of provider and clinical staff time per calendar month for a single high-risk condition.

- CMS explained in the CY 2021 Medicare Physician Fee Schedule Final Rule that the Principle Care Management services codes will be replaced with CPT codes in CY 2022.

Chapter

10

Advance Care
Planning (ACP)

Advance Care Planning (ACP) is a face-to-face conversation between a qualified healthcare provider and the caregiver or patient to discuss the patient's health care desires if they become unable to make decisions regarding their care. Advance Care Planning may include a detailed description of advance directives like standard forms, with or without completing the forms. CMS expects ACP will be billed every time there is a pertinent change in the patient's health condition or the provider spends time directing a discussion that supports the caregiver/patient as they decide and document their end-of-life priorities.

- Advance Care Planning must be voluntary, and the provider must document the caregiver or patient's advance consent to voluntarily contribute to the advance care planning discussion. CMS also expects and encourages providers to make the patient aware of possible applicable cost-sharing when this takes place outside of an annual wellness visit.

- ACP must be face-to-face encounters and only involve the time consumed discussing the patient priorities and advance directives; time consumed on other aspects of the encounter cannot be considered towards this service component.

- Major examples of standard forms may include a living will, physician's orders for life-sustaining treatment (POLST), power of attorney for healthcare, and physician's orders for scope of treatment (POST).

- Advance Care Planning may be billed in combination with AWV, CCM, E/M, and/or TCM.

- The documentation for ACP must include the discussion details and the accurate time consumed discussing advance directives.

- CPT 99497: recommended for Advance care planning including the discussion and explanation of advance directives provided by the physician or other qualified healthcare provider. It should be reported for a face-to-face encounter with the patient, family members, or/ and surrogate in the first 30 minutes.

- CPT 99498: should be used for Advance care planning including the discussion and explanation of advance directives such as standard forms, delivered by the physician or other qualified healthcare provider for each additional 30 minutes.

- Advance care planning is also on Medicare's approved list of telehealth services. Therefore, ACP services can be delivered and billed via telehealth. It's also one of the specific telehealth services that can be rendered via audio-only (phone call) and does not need the application of video to bill for the discussion.

Chapter

11

Prolonged Services without Contacting the Patient Directly

⚙️

Prolonged Services without contacting the patient directly are applicable when a qualified healthcare provider (MD, DO, PA, and NP) consumes time that links to an E/M face-to-face encounter but goes above and beyond the normal time corresponding with that CPT code. Medicare will provide reimbursement for non-face-to-face prolonged services delivered to an E/M visit. This enables health care providers to be billed for time consumed reviewing extensive medical records or prolonged telephone time talking about history or the patient's medical problem in advance of, or after, the encounter.

- CPT 99358: recommended for prolonged E/M service before and/or after direct patient care, initial hour. At least 31 minutes is essential to bill

- CPT 99359: this is an additional code for CPT 99358 and can be reported for prolonged service delivered for every extra 30 minutes (after the first hour)

- Prolonged Services Without contacting the Patient directly must be above and beyond the usual effort and time a physician or qualified health care provider would consume with the patient, and why the service went beyond the usual effort and time must be documented.

- It cannot be billed for services that can be linked with more specific codes without having an upper time limit like care plan oversight, online medical evaluations, and team conferences.

- The time consumed can be after, on, or before the date of the face-to-face encounter, however, services must be linked to an E/M encounter. Documentation must explain what was assessed or reviewed and how the time was used.

- It requires both initiating and stop times, the total time, and DOS (date of service) to be recorded in the medical record; the time does not essentially require to be continuous; however, it must take place on the same calendar date.

- According to CMS guidance, you should check with your local MAC (Medicare Administrative Contractor) for additional documentation needs.

- Prolonged Services Without contacting the Patient directly is bundled, which means it cannot be billed within the same calendar month as the following services:

  ▪ Care Plan Oversight (G0181, G0182)

  ▪ INR Monitoring Services (93792, 93793)

  ▪ Online Digital E/M (99421, 99422, 99423)

  ▪ General Behavioral Health Integration Services (BHI) (99484)

  ▪ Chronic Care Management (99487-9/ 99490/99491)

  ▪ BHI Integrated Care Management (99492, 99493, 99494).

- Prolonged Services CPT 99354, 99355, 99358, and 99359 are also recommended in the domiciliary, home, skilled nursing, inpatient, and observation hospital settings.

Chapter

12

Prolonged Services with Contacting the Patient Directly

👩‍⚕️

Prolonged services with contacting the patient directly are applicable when a qualifying healthcare provider (MD, DO, PA, and NP) consumes extra face-to-face time with the patient that goes above and beyond the usual CPT code threshold time for that specific service. Medicare will provide reimbursement for prolonged services when the patient is contacted directly for services in the inpatient, outpatient or home care setting that go above and beyond the normal service. This is recommended to use when the total face-to-face time consumed by the provider or other qualified health care professional exceeds the normal time assigned to the base evaluation and management code by a minimum of 30 minutes.

- Prolonged services are actually add-on codes and must be billed with their companion evaluation and management codes.

- These are time-based services; therefore, the accurate time spent during face-to-face visits with the patient and/or caregiver must be recorded in the medical record.

- Time does not essentially need to be continuous; however, it must take place on the same calendar date. The encounter must be direct face-to-face that is beyond and above the average visit time of the code billed.

- Documentation must thoroughly explain why the visit went above and beyond the usual service time.

- CPT 99354: CPT 99354 is reported for prolonged E/M or psychotherapy services, beyond and above the average primary procedure service time, the first hour.

- CPT 99355: CPT 99355 is recommended for prolonged E/M or psychotherapy, with each additional 30 minutes.

Chapter

13

Cognitive Evaluation and Care Plan Services

Cognitive evaluation and care plan services is a thorough assessment for a new or established patient who shows signs and/or symptoms of cognitive impairment, and for whom the etiology, diagnosis, or intensity of their problem needs to be confirmed or established. Medicare provides reimbursement to physicians and other qualified health care providers for an assessment of a patient with cognitive impairment.

CPT 99483: recommended for evaluation and care planning for a patient with cognitive impairment who needs an independent assessment in the office or other outpatient setting such as rest home or home that can be reported once every 180 days per provider.

CPT 99483 needs the following 10 specific service components to be delivered and documented:

1. Cognitive-focused assessment, including specific history and examination

2. MDM (Medical decision-making) of modest or severe complexity

3. Functional assessment for basic as well as instrumental activities of daily living, including decision-making capability

4. Use of standardized and recommended equipment for staging dementia (i.e., clinical dementia rating or functional evaluation staging test)

5. Appropriate medication reconciliation as well reviewing for high-risk medications

6. Assessment for neuropsychiatric and behavioral features, including anxiety and depression, via a standardized or recommended screening tool

7. Assessment of safety like home environment, including operation of a motor vehicle

8. Recognition of the caregiver's needs, social support, knowledge, needs, and readiness to

take on caregiving tasks

9. Establishment, review, updating, or revision of an advance care plan

10. Development of a written care plan, including initial plans to manage any neurocognitive symptoms, neuropsychiatric features, functional restrictions, and referral to community resources as required (e.g., rehabilitation centers, adult day care programs, support groups). Remember that the written care plan should always be shared with the caregiver or/and patient with initial support and education.

CPT 99483 may NOT be billed in combination with an E/M or CCM code. The usual face-to-face time consumed with the caregiver or/and patient is 50 minutes.

Chapter

14

Counseling Services Regarding Smoking Cessation

This is a service in which the healthcare professional counsels the patient on the significance of stopping tobacco use. Most private insurers and Medicare will provide reimbursement to physicians and other qualified health care providers for counseling patients about the cessation of tobacco use. The provider must report and document a diagnosis of tobacco usage and may report two individual cessation encounters per 12-month period. Remember that each reporting visit may include a maximum of four intensive or moderate sessions, with a total benefit of eight sessions annually.

Documentation of smoking cessation and counseling services must include the following components:

- The accurate amount of time consumed on cessation counseling (at least four minutes to bill)

- Brief and comprehensive description of the nature of the counseling encounter and the patient's willingness to discontinue using tobacco products

- If reported in conjunction with another service, you must explain how this was different from the other service delivered

- CPT 99406: recommended for smoking and tobacco use cessation counseling encounter, intermediate in nature, more than three minutes, and up to 10 minutes

- CPT 99407: used for smoking and tobacco use cessation counseling encounter, intensive in nature, and more than 10 minutes

- The patient must have a valid diagnosis of ICD 10 F17.2xx that represents "Nicotine dependence, unspecified, cigarettes, chewing tobacco, other" or Z87.891 that describes "Personal history of nicotine dependence" to qualify for reimbursement.

- Document the specific tobacco use of the patient, your counseling for cessation, and the negative health effects of smoking, evaluating the patient's willingness to smoking cessation behavior, recommending a specific change, and setting a quit date.

Chapter

15

Screening, Brief Intervention, and Referral to Treatment (SBIRT) Services

S BIRT services are an evidence-based approaches to rendering early intervention and management services for individuals with substance use disorders, and those at higher risk of establishing a substance use disorder. Screening, Brief Intervention, and Referral to Treatment (SBIRT) Services are intended for early intervention for individuals with non-dependent substance use to support them before more advanced and extensive treatment is required.

- Eligible healthcare professionals who can bill for SBIRT services include Physicians (MDs and Dos), Nurse Practitioners (NPs), Physician Assistants (PA), Clinical Psychologist (CP), Clinical Nurse Specialist (CNS), Certified Nurse Midwife (CNM), Clinical Social Worker (CSW), and Independently Practicing Psychologists (IPPs).

- There are three basic components of SBIRT Services, which are described below:

  - Screening: Evaluate or screen the patient via a Medicare Structured Assessment Tool to find out the severity and proper treatment. You may utilize tools that include the W.H.O's Alcohol Use Disorders Identification Test (AUDIT) and the Drug Abuse Screening Test (DAST).

  - Brief Intervention: Focus on increasing awareness and delivering appropriate insight on substance use and motivation for positive behavior change. These are brief discussions where the qualified healthcare professional increases awareness and provides feedback, advice, and motivation. Medicare reimburses up to five counseling sessions.

- Referral to Treatment: Refer patients whose evaluation represents a need for additional management to specialty care.

Reporting and documentation for each patient visit must include:

- Beginning and terminating times or whole face-to-face time with the patient

- The patient's initial response to changes in management, progress, and diagnosis revision

- The reason for ordering diagnostic and other ancillary services or to make sure it is easily implied

- Evaluation, diagnosis, and clinical impression

- Physical examination findings and results of previous diagnostic tests

- Plan of care

- Reason for the visit and related history

- Identification of appropriate health risk factors

- Making present and past diagnoses accessible for the consulting and treating physicians

HCPCS G2011: recommended for structured assessment and brief intervention of 5–14 minutes, related to Alcohol or/and substance abuse other than tobacco

HCPCS G0396: recommended for structured assessment and brief intervention of 15–30 minutes, related to Alcohol or/and substance abuse other than tobacco

HCPCS G0397: use for structured assessment and brief intervention of more than 30 minutes related to Alcohol or/and substance abuse other than tobacco

Chapter

16

Anticoagulation Management

A nticoagulation Management is the surveillance and monitoring of PT/INR (Prothrombin Time International Normalized Ratio) for patients on long-term Coumadin, Warfarin, and other oral-anticoagulants. Medicare will provide reimbursement to physicians and other qualified healthcare providers for outpatient and home-based International Normalized Ratio (INR) monitoring services in anticoagulation management (Nicoletti, 2021).

The two advanced services available are as:

CPT 93792: used for the training the patient and/or caregiver for initial set-up when a patient is placed on a home International Normalized Ratio (INR) monitoring regimen. This service can be rendered under the supervision and direction of a physician or qualified healthcare provider.

Documentation of CPT 93792 requires:

- It must be a face-to-face encounter

- It must include patient education on care and use for the INR monitor, receiving a blood sample, and directions for reporting home INR test results

- Documentation of the ability of the patient or/and caregiver to perform testing and report test results

CPT 93793: recommended for review and subsequent management of a new office, home, or lab test once per day irrespective of the number of tests reviewed. Remember, this code is not billable with an E/M service. Documentation of CPT 93793 requires:

- Reviewing and interpretation of test results

- May also include test results along with patient instructions and dosage adjustment, if essential

- Scheduling of more tests when required

Neither 93793 nor 93792 are billable with transitional care management and/or chronic care management services because PT/INR monitoring is considered included in TCM and/or CCM services.

Chapter

17

General Behavioral Health Integration (BHI) and Care Management Services

General behavioral health integration (BHI) and care management services are recommended for billing monthly services rendered by delivering integrated behavioral health and primary care services.

CPT 99484: should be used to report a minimum of 20 minutes of care management services for a behavioral health problem in a calendar month. It can be coordinated work performed by a billing provider and clinical staff. Medicare expects 15 minutes to be spent by the billing practitioner. Please refer to the Medicare Learning Network17 for full details. Service components for CPT 99484 include the following:

- Systematic evaluation and monitoring with the use of standard and applicable validated rating scale; if initial evaluation is needed, it may be billed separately

- Care planning with the patient and the primary care team, with revision if the problem is not improving

- Continuous professional relationship with a dedicated member of the care team

- Coordination and facilitation of behavioral health treatment

- Advance patient consent, either written or verbal, is essential and must be reported in the medical record to make sure the patient knows and is aware of applicable cost-sharing.

- Requirements for service and documentation of CPT 99484 include evaluating or monitoring the patient, establishing and revising the care plan, facilitating and coordinating treatment with the patient and involved parties, and maintaining an ongoing positive relationship with a designated member of the care team.

- General BHI (99484) and traditional CCM services (CPT 99490) may sometimes be submitted by the same provider in the same calendar month if different care management services are rendered. Effort and time should be counted once towards either activity to prevent double-counting time for the same type of effort.

- You should also explore Psychiatric Collaborative Care Management Services (CoCM) if your practice includes a psychiatric consultant and behavioral health care manager. Psychiatric Collaborative Care Management Services (CoCM) services should be reported with CPT codes 99492 - 99494 and HCPCS G2214 for the time spent by the behavioral care manager.

Additional Major Coding Updates

1. As of 01/01/19, CMS eliminated the requirement for providers to report and explain why a patient is being seen in the home rather than the office if the encounter is clinically essential. This means providers are no longer required to report in their progress notes why a patient was seen in the home instead of the office. The decision to

see the patient in the home is left to the patient or/and provider.

2. As of 01/01/19, Medicare provides reimbursement for interprofessional internet consultation codes. Interprofessional internet consultation services must be requested formally by the treating or attending provider. Consultations are just payable for those providers who are allowed to bill E/M services. The consulting provider should always be from a different specialty than the requesting provider.

3. CMS explained their broad policy that billing providers (physicians, physician assistants, nurse practitioners) and some non-physician providers, including therapists, can verify and review documentation reported in the medical record by the designated medical team members for their own rendered services reimbursed under the physician fee schedule. This policy may include students working under the supervision of a provider who delivers and bills Medicare directly for their services as long as the documentation is verified and reviewed by the billing provider.

4. For the duration of the COVID-19 public health emergency or through December 31, 2021 (whichever is later), to minimize the infection exposure, CMS changed the definition of direct supervision and included virtual availability of the supervising practitioner or physician via interactive video and audio real-time communications technology.

Chapter

18

Interprofessional Internet Consultation Services

Interprofessional Internet Consultation Services include interprofessional internet/telephone/ electronic health record evaluation and management services rendered by a consultative physician, including a written and verbal report to the treating/requesting provider of the patient:

99446: used for 5-10 minutes of clinical consultative discussion and review

99447: recommended for 11-20 minutes of clinical consultative discussion and review

99448: used for 21-30 minutes of medical consultative discussion and review

99449: recommended for 31 minutes or above of medical consultative discussion and review

CPT 99451: reported for interprofessional internet/telephone/electronic health record evaluation and management service rendered by a consultative physician including a written report to the treating/requesting physician or other qualified healthcare providers of the patient, which involves five or more minutes of medical consultative time.

CPT 99452: recommended for interprofessional internet/telephone/electronic health record referral services rendered by a requesting or treating physician or other qualified healthcare providers. It should be reported when 16 to 30 minutes were consumed in preparing the referral or/and discussing with the consulting provider.

CPT codes 99451 and 99452 differ from the other interprofessional consults services codes because the report was written so they do not need a verbal and written medical discussion.

4

Assertive Community Treatment and Home Health Care Psychiatric Services

Chapter

19

Assertive Community Treatment (ACT)

Assertive Community Treatment or ACT is an evidence-based method of caring for people with severe, complex mental health problems. Assertive Community Treatment has been shown to minimize emergency visits and hospitalization for patients with hard-to-treat psychosis and other psychosocial instabilities (Sood & Owen, 2014). Assertive Community Treatment is a specific intervention approach involving a multi-disciplinary team with flexible scheduling, care in the community, and crisis management.

ACT teams work on multiple different approaches to help individuals achieve psychosocial stability and eventually, their own recovery goals. The basic philosophy of Assertive community treatment is to provide the required support to facilitate keeping an individual well outside the hospital. ACT clients are usually people with psychotic problems who also show remarkable psycho-social instability. They often possess treatment-resistant features, personality problems, substance use disorders, and poor coping skills. They usually have histories of repeated hospitalizations, itinerancy, and legal involvement.

To meet the requirements of these clients, ACT teams employ psycho-educators, social workers, substance abuse specialists, and vocational specialists as well as qualified nurses and psychiatrists (Woesner et al., 2014). Specific interventions provided by the ACT team may range from biological (providing support in managing physical conditions, medication supervision) to psychological (motivational interviewing, CBT), and social support. ACT teams provide support in almost all aspects of their client's lives and meet them wherever they can—at their homes, at the hospital, or in the community settings. ACT teams may also remain involved when their clients are admitted to the hospital or even visit emergency rooms.

ACT Locations

ACT has already been implemented in developed countries like the United States, Australia, Canada, and the U.K. In the United States, Assertive community treatment was implemented by the Department of Veterans Affairs across the country.

Assertive community treatment is a specific intervention approach in which services are not rendered in a clinic, but rather in community locations, in the patient's home, in homeless shelters, or wherever is most convenient and easy for the client using the service.

ACT Team

The ACT team is a group of direct service staff members who individually have a wide range of clinical skills and rehabilitation expertise to provide appropriate person-centered and recovery-oriented outreach mental health services. Different tasks of the ACT team members are assigned by the team leader. These team members, along with the psychiatric prescriber, work collaboratively with a client and his/her family and arrange subsequent person-directed recovery planning meetings. The ACT team size may vary and ranges from 50 to 120 staff members, maintained at the recommended ratio of 1:10.

The core members of an ACT team include a primary care manager, a nurse, the psychiatric prescriber, and a rehabilitation or clinical staff member who shares case coordination and service provision activities with each member of the team. The team has an ongoing responsibility to be aware of the client's life, desires, circumstances, and goals; to coordinate with the client to establish and write the recovery plan; to offer different choices and options in the recovery plan; to make immediate modifications according to the client's requirements; and to advocate for the client's rights, wishes, and priorities.

The ACT team is responsible for delivering much of the client's treatment, rehabilitation tasks, and support services. Team members are assigned different tasks and separate service roles with the client, as recommended in the person-directed recovery plan.

Services Provided by the ACT Team

The ACT team delivers comprehensive evaluation, treatment, rehabilitation services, and support activities including:

- Assisting the client with housing needs as necessary
- Accessing appropriate medical care

- Substance use counseling or/and easy access to treatment
- Skill building and other life skills support services
- Medication delivery services
- Assisting with grocery shopping
- Connecting the client to different community resources
- Transporting the client to medical appointments
- Encouraging and supporting the client to choose a healthy lifestyle, engage in proper personal hygiene, encourage long and short-term goal-setting and money management
- Connecting the client to income assistance services
- Evaluate for medical issues and refer them to the client's family doctor or local medical clinic
- Assist the client in managing his/her medication if essential

It is estimated that almost 75 percent of the services that ACT teams deliver are offered in community settings that are convenient and comfortable for the client e.g. the client's home, coffee shops/local restaurants, shelters, parks, or even shelters if that's where the client prefers.

ACT teams work closely and collaboratively with clients and their families or other support groups preferred by the client to develop a recovery plan for improving quality of life and reducing time spent in emergency hospital visits and hospital admissions.

The Major Principles of ACT

- ACT is more of a service-delivery model rather than a case management program.

- The primary purpose of ACT is recovery by using community treatment and rehabilitation services.

- ACT is characterized by:

  - A team approach model

  - Services are provided in the areas and contexts where they are required (in-vivo service delivery approach)

  - A small caseload with a staff-to-client ratio of about 1 to 10

  - A service is continued as long as required (time-unlimited services)

  - A shared caseload as the team as a whole is responsible for making sure that clients receive the services they require to live in the community and to achieve their personal goals.

- ▪ A flexible service delivery approach
- ▪ A fixed point of responsibility that means instead of sending clients to several providers for services, the ACT team delivers the services that clients need in their homes and other community settings.
- ▪ 24/7 services availability
- ● ACT is for people with persistent and challenging problems.

Chapter

20

Home Health Care Psychiatric Services

Patients suffering from a diagnosed psychiatric disorder may require evaluation, psychotherapy, and counseling services by a psychiatrically trained staff or skilled nursing members. Patients may also need occupational therapy, medical social services, home health aide services, or other home health services regarding the management of their psychiatric disorder.

Home healthcare psychiatric services provide comprehensive psychiatric services in the comfort of a client's home. These services strive to:

- Prevent frequent hospitalizations

- Enhance access to mental health services
- Provide follow-ups
- Support families in improving their quality of life

In-home healthcare psychiatric services and psychiatric nurses collaborate with primary care providers or/and psychiatrists to provide patient-centered psychiatric care as needed.

Services are usually based on a comprehensive psychological, physical, cognitive, mental, family, and environmental evaluation of the patient within the home. Relevant interventions are delivered by certified, licensed clinical nurse specialists or by qualified nurses with pertinent experience in psychiatric nursing. Psychiatric home services may include:

- Psychiatric nursing assessments and consultations
- Psycho-awareness approaches with the patient or/and caregiver family to increase the patient's level of awareness and control over the illness, and improve coping skills through:
  - Symptom management
  - Medication education

- Appropriate coping skills
- Effective communication skills
- Proper monitoring and management of medication administration
- Venipuncture and regular monitoring of the level of psychotropic medications in the blood
- Post-hospitalization follow-up to assist in bridging the gap between the patient's transition from hospital to community
- Identification, collaboration, and mobilization of the supports required to maintain the patient in the community
- Appropriate therapeutic interventions, including:
  - Psychosocial
  - A variety of relaxation techniques
  - Supportive therapy
  - Clinical case management
  - Counseling of the patient and family
- Psychotherapy services that may include:
  - Behavioral
  - Cognitive
  - Brief therapy

- Dynamic
- Family therapy
- Crisis intervention
- Proper support and education of the caregiver

Chapter

21

Billing and Reimbursement opportunities for the Psychiatric CoCM and General BHI

Since January 2017, the CMS has approved payment for services rendered to patients with behavioral health problems who are receiving behavioral health integration services or attending psychiatric collaborative care programs. CMS has grouped these services as "Behavioral Health Integration" (BHI) services, which include four codes demonstrating "Psychiatric Collaborative Care Management services (CoCM)" (99492, 99493, 99494, and HCPCS G2214) and one code describing "General BHI service" (99484). These services cover patients with behavioral health problems or substance use disorder. These services may be billed in both facility and non-facility settings. These services are also covered in Rural Health Clinics (RHCs) and Federally Qualified Health Centers (FQHCs) settings. American Psychiatric Association (APA) encourages private payers to embrace these codes as well.

Psychiatric Collaborative Care Management (CoCM)

Psychiatric CoCM is typically delivered by a primary care team consisting of a care manager and a primary care physician who provide services in collaboration with a psychiatric consultant like a psychiatrist. Psychiatric CoCM is mainly directed by the primary care team, which includes structured care management with frequent evaluations of clinical status via recommended tools and modification of management as appropriate. The psychiatrist renders regular consultations to the primary care team to analyze the clinical status and care of patients and to make further recommendations (American Medical Association, 2021).

The following codes are recommended to bill for psychiatric CoCM in all settings except RHCs and FQHCs:

CPT 99492: recommended for initial psychiatric collaborative care management services provided for the initial 70 minutes in the first calendar month of behavioral health care manager services in collaboration with a psychiatric consultant and supervised by the treating physician or other qualified health care provider.

CPT 99492 services require:

- Appropriate participation and involvement of the patient in the treatment plan by the treating physician or other qualified health care professional

- Initial evaluation and screening of patient through recommended screening/evaluation tools

- Establishment of a personalized and customized treatment plan for the patient

- Weekly consultation by the psychiatrist

- Consultation by the psychiatrist on review and revision of the treatment plan as needed

- Updating registry with the proper patient follow-up and latest status by behavioral health care manager

- Application of evidence-based methods like motivational interviewing, behavioral activation, and other focused treatment strategies

CPT 99493: used for subsequent psychiatric collaborative care management services provided for the first 60 minutes in a subsequent month of behavioral health care manager services in collaboration with a psychiatrist and supervised by the treating physician or other qualified health care provider.

CPT 99493 services require:

- Updating the registry with proper patient follow-up and latest status by behavioral health care manager

- Weekly consultation by the psychiatrist

- Ongoing collaboration with the treating physician or other qualified health care professional along with other relevant treating mental health clinicians

- Consultation by the psychiatrist on review and revision of the treatment plan as needed

- Application of evidence-based methods like motivational interviewing, behavioral activation, and other focused treatment methodologies

- Monitoring of patient progress through recommended screening tools

CPT 99494: recommended for initial or subsequent psychiatric collaborative care management services provided for each additional 30 minutes in a calendar month of behavioral health care manager services in collaboration with a psychiatrist and supervised by the treating physician or other qualified health care provider.

HCPCS G2214: recommended when billing for initial or subsequent psychiatric collaborative care management services provided for the initial 30 minutes in first or subsequent month of behavioral health care manager services in collaboration with a psychiatrist and supervised by the treating physician or other qualified health care provider. This code was established by CMS on January 1, 2021, in response to meeting the need of having an additional code that would indicate shorter intervals of time spent with the patient.

General BHI

CMS developed a code to represent general care management services for those patients who have behavioral health problems.

CPT 99484: recommended for care management services for behavioral health problems provided for a minimum of 20 minutes of clinical staff time supervised by a physician or other qualified health care provider, per calendar month. This code requires:

- Initial evaluation or follow-up monitoring involving the utilization of recommended rating scales.

- Appropriate behavioral health care planning in conjunction with psychiatric/ behavioral health issues, including revision for patients who are not improving or progressing.

- Collaborating and facilitating treatment such as psychotherapy, counseling or/and psychiatric consultation, and pharmacotherapy.

- Continuity of care with a dedicated team member of the care team.

Section

5

The Future of Home Health Care

While the future of the home health industry is bright, it is surely not without some unexpected challenges. Experts in the home health industry are expecting some dramatic overhauls to the Medicare Home Health Benefit. However, changing policy frameworks, consolidation concerns, and technology adoptions are some of the hurdles that the home health care industry faces in both the long and short term. But as the home health industry learns to function amidst the new normal of a Covid-19 public health emergency, there have never been higher demands for home health care options or acknowledgment of the power of care rendered in the home, whether virtually or in-person.

If there was any uncertainty before, the home health care industry now most definitely has a proper place at healthcare's table. Only time will decide what the next few years and months will hold, but the future of home-based care is brighter than ever before.

References

1. Office of Regulatory Affairs. (2018, September 14). *Medical Device Overview*. U.S. Food and Drug Administration. https://www.fda.gov/industry/regulated-products/medical-device-overview

2. American Medical Association. (2021, August 17). *Learn about 4 new CPT codes to bill for collaborative care*. https://www.ama-assn.org/practice-management/cpt/learn-about-4-new-cpt-codes-bill-collaborative-care

3. Brunton, S. A. (2021). Telemedicine: The 2020 House Call. *Clinical Diabetes*, *39*(1), 13. https://doi.org/10.2337/cd20-0106

4. *CMS NEWS ALERT APRIL 6, 2020 | CMS*. (2020, April 6). Www.Cms.Gov. https://www.cms.gov/newsroom/press-releases/cms-news-alert-april-6-2020

5. *Coronavirus Disease 2019 (COVID-19)*. (2020, February 11). Centers for Disease Control and Prevention. https://www.cdc.gov/coronavirus/2019-ncov/global-covid-19/handwashing.html

6. *A Guide to Providing In-Home Visiting Services During the COVID-19 Pandemic*. (2020, December 15). Wisconsin Department of Health Services. https://www.dhs.wisconsin.gov/library/p-02853.htm

7. *Healthcare Workers*. (2020a, February 11). Centers for Disease Control and Prevention. https://www.cdc.gov/coronavirus/2019-ncov/hcp/non-us-settings/overview/index.htm

8. *Healthcare Workers*. (2020b, February 11). Centers for Disease Control and Prevention. https://www.cdc.gov/coronavirus/2019-ncov/hcp/using-ppe.html

9. History.com Editors. (2021, February 23). *First confirmed case of COVID-19 found in U.S.* HISTORY. https://www.history.com/this-day-in-history/first-confirmed-case-of-coronavirus-found-in-us-washington-state

10. *The Home Health Sector Responds to the COVID-19 Crisis*. (2020, December 3). Partnership for Quality Home Healthcare. https://pqhh.org/covid-19/

11. *Implications for Home-Based Care Providers in the CY 2021 Medicare Physician Fee Schedule (MPFS) Final Rule*. (2021, February 12). Home Centered Care Institute. https://www.hccinstitute.org/implications-for-home-based-care-providers-in-the-cy-2021-medicare-physician-fee-schedule-mpfs-final-rule/

12. Johnston, R., Kobb, R. F., Marty, C., & McVeigh, P. (2021). VA Video Telehealth and Training Programs during the COVID-19 Response. *Telehealth and Medicine Today*. Published. https://doi.org/10.30953/tmt.v6.241

13. Khoshrounejad, F., Hamednia, M., Mehrjerd, A., Pichaghsaz, S., Jamalirad, H., Sargolzaei, M., Hoseini, B., & Aalaei, S. (2021). Telehealth-Based Services during the

COVID-19 Pandemic: A Systematic Review of Features and Challenges. *Frontiers in Public Health*, *9*. https://doi.org/10.3389/fpubh.2021.711762

14. Kichloo, A., Albosta, M., Dettloff, K., Wani, F., El-Amir, Z., Singh, J., Aljadah, M., Chakinala, R. C., Kanugula, A. K., Solanki, S., & Chugh, S. (2020). Telemedicine, the current COVID-19 pandemic and the future: a narrative review and perspectives moving forward in the USA. *Family Medicine and Community Health*, *8*(3), e000530. https://doi.org/10.1136/fmch-2020-000530

15. *List of Telehealth Services | CMS*. (2021, August 17). CMS. https://www.cms.gov/Medicare/Medicare-General-Information/Telehealth/Telehealth-Codes

16. *MLN home page | CMS*. (2021, June 28). The Medicare Learning Network. https://www.cms.gov/Outreach-and-Education/Medicare-Learning-Network-MLN/MLNGenInfo

17. Morens, D. M., Breman, J. G., Calisher, C. H., Doherty, P. C., Hahn, B. H., Keusch, G. T., Kramer, L. D., LeDuc, J. W., Monath, T. P., & Taubenberger, J. K. (2020). The Origin of COVID-19 and Why It Matters. *The American Journal of Tropical Medicine and Hygiene*, *103*(3), 955–959. https://doi.org/10.4269/ajtmh.20-0849

18. Nicoletti, B. (2021, August 18). *Anticoagulation Management*. CodingIntel. https://codingintel.com/anticoagulation-management/

19. *Overview of the Medicare Physician Fee Schedule Search | CMS*. (2021, July 1). CMS. https://www.cms.gov/medicare/physician-fee-schedule/search/overview

20. Prevounce Health. (2021). *A Comprehensive Guide to Remote Patient Monitoring.* Https://Www.Prevounce. Com/. https://www.prevounce.com/a-comprehensive-guide-to-remote-patient-monitoring

21. Rogers, J. (2021). Coding telehealth services during COVID-19. *The Nurse Practitioner*, *46*(2), 10–12. https://doi.org/10.1097/01.npr.0000731584.40074.eb

22. Shereen, M. A., Khan, S., Kazmi, A., Bashir, N., & Siddique, R. (2020). COVID-19 infection: Emergence, transmission, and characteristics of human coronaviruses. *Journal of Advanced Research*, *24*, 91–98. https://doi.org/10.1016/j.jare.2020.03.005

23. Sood, L., & Owen, A. (2014). A 10-year service evaluation of an assertive community treatment team: trends in hospital bed use. *Journal of Mental Health*, *23*(6), 323–327. https://doi.org/10.3109/09638237.2014.954694

24. Statista. (2021, September 6). *Cumulative cases of COVID-19 worldwide from Jan. 22, 2020 to Sep. 5, 2021, by day.* https://www.statista.com/statistics/1103040/cumulative-coronavirus-covid19-cases-number-worldwide-by-day/

25. *Tools and Tip Sheets.* (2021). Home Centered Care Institute. https://www.hccinstitute.org/hccintelligence/tools-and-tip-sheets/

26. Woesner, M. E., Marsh, J., & Kanofsky, J. D. (2014). The Assertive Community Treatment Team. *The Primary Care Companion for CNS Disorders*. Published. https://doi.org/10.4088/pcc.14br01639